Cryptocurrency ICO Investing: A Guide to Understanding ICO Investing

Book #6 of the book series by Cryptomasher

Sean Bennett

Table of Contents

Introduction..5
Chapter 1: All About ICOs..6
Chapter 2: Investing in ICOs....................................15
Chapter 3: Mindset for Investing.............................23
Chapter 4: Paying Taxes on Your Profits................32
Conclusion..36

© Copyright 2018 by **Cryptomasher** - All rights reserved.

The follow eBook is reproduced below with the goal of providing information that is as accurate and reliable as possible. Regardless, purchasing this eBook can be seen as consent to the fact that both the publisher and the author of this book are in no way experts on the topics discussed within and that any recommendations or suggestions that are made herein are for entertainment purposes only. Professionals should be consulted as needed prior to undertaking any of the action endorsed herein.

This declaration is deemed fair and valid by both the American Bar Association and the Committee of Publishers Association and is legally binding throughout the United States.

Furthermore, the transmission, duplication or reproduction of any of the following work including specific information will be considered an illegal act irrespective of if it is done electronically or in print. This extends to creating a secondary or tertiary copy of the work or a recorded copy and is only allowed with express written consent from the Publisher. All additional right reserved.

The information in the following pages is broadly considered to be a truthful and accurate account of facts and as such any inattention, use or misuse of the information in question by the reader will render any resulting actions solely under their purview. There are no scenarios in which the publisher or the original author of this work can be in any fashion deemed liable for any hardship or damages that may befall them after undertaking information described herein.

Additionally, the information in the following pages is intended only for informational purposes and should thus be thought of as universal. As befitting its nature, it is presented without assurance regarding its prolonged validity or interim quality. Trademarks that are mentioned are done without written consent and can in no way be considered an endorsement from the trademark holder.

Introduction

Congratulations on downloading *Cryptocurrency ICO Investing: A Guide to Understanding ICO Investing* and thank you for doing so. While the opportunity to invest in Bitcoin while it was under the $100 mark may have passed you by, there are plenty of new cryptocurrencies on the horizon just waiting to take the world by storm, bringing profits to its early adopters in the process. Initial coin offerings are a great way to get in on the ground floor of one of these new cryptocurrencies by ensuring that you will pay the best possible price for the cryptocurrency in question in exchange for taking on additional risk.

Separating the wheat from the chaff when it comes to future ICOs can be easier said than done which is why the following chapters will discuss everything you need to know to see a successful ICO investment through to fruition. You will start by learning all about ICOs and the many pros and cons associated with investing in them. Once you have decided that ICOs are, in fact, for you, you will then learn everything you need to know about making a wise investment, as well as what you need to do in order to actually take the plunge and invest in your first ICO.

From there you will learn all about the proper mindset required for investing in ICOs successfully as well as when to hold on for dear life and when to cut your losses. Finally, you will learn all about the unique issues that investing in an ICO raises when it comes to paying taxes.

There are plenty of books on this subject on the market, thanks again for choosing this one! Every effort was made to ensure it is full of as much useful information as possible, please enjoy!

Chapter 1: All About ICOs

In this chapter you will learn...

- What are ICOs
- ICOs and blockchain
- ICOs and altcoins

While a vast majority of the talk in the cryptocurrency space has been around Bitcoin since it first broke onto the scene in 2009, 2018 is looking increasingly like the year that will buck this trend once and for all. As of March 2018, there are nearly 1,500 different cryptocurrencies on the market, with more coming online each week. From an investment standpoint, this means that there are already plenty of potentially viable alternatives to Bitcoin out there with plenty of more potential money makers on the horizon.

What are ICOs?

These days, the primary way that new cryptocurrencies break into the scene is through what is known as an initial coin offering (ICO). While the name comes from the initial public offering that a company will go through when it goes public for the first time, the two activities are quite different. When utilizing an initial coin offering, the company that is planning to release the cryptocurrency does so at an extremely low rate as a means of funding either the release of, or less ideally the creation of, the cryptocurrency in question. Those who invest early are taking a risk that the new coins they buy will ultimately jump to a price that is greater than what they initially paid once it hits the market.

In fact, other than a similar naming convention, the ICO and the IPO have very little in common with one another. The IPO is an extremely measured process that is known for the amount of red tape the company in question is required to jump through in order for its stock to be listed on an open exchange. Additionally, when they buy into an IPO, investors are trading their cash for equity, as well as possible voting rights, based on the type of stock they purchased. Finally, the entire process is watched extremely closely by the Securities and Exchange Commission to ensure that nothing illegal is taking place.

The ICO process is not bogged down by nearly as much regulation. This starts right from the beginning as the amount of information you can expect to find on a new potential ICO is going to vary dramatically from project to project with some having detailed analysis of the market and how their cryptocurrency fills an existing need, and others having little more than a white paper and pitch about a utopia where everyone uses their cryptocurrency to get along. Regardless of the promises that are made, it is important to keep in mind that investors are investing to fund the future of the project of the ICO.

Those who have found success with ICOs in the past, or who are very positive on cryptocurrency in general, can argue that the process is like an accelerated form of venture capitalism and point to success in the market such as Ethereum to back them up. If you have not heard of Ethereum, it is likely the second biggest name in the cryptocurrency space. While Bitcoin focuses almost exclusively on P2P payment transactions, Ethereum has instead focused on creating a platform for people to utilize smart contracts to the fullest. To learn more about smart contracts see my other book **Blockchain: A Guide to Understanding Blockchain.**

While it has since shied away from the term, Ethereum was actually funded though what would be today called an ICO, though the term was not in common usage when it first came onto the scene. The initial sale of its currency, ether, took place in the summer of 2014 and gave the Ethereum team the capital they needed to ensure that Ethereum would launch successfully in 2015 with more than 12 million coins already in circulation. Ethereum created many millionaires of its early adopters. Ethereum was approximately 30 cents an ether at

ICO which goes to show how millions have been made through it.

Another, more current, example is Wanchian which was created by one of the programmers who created Factom, a cryptocurrency which is now worth around $200 million. Besides offering its own type of cryptocurrency, known as wancoin, Wanchain provides users with the ability to connect to a wide variety of different blockchains, making it the first time that true interoperability within the cryptocurrency space is truly possible. Wanchain's ICO took place in Oct. 2017 and all of its early access coins, 210,000,000 in all, sold out, raising a total of approximately $36 million.

The first-ever ICO took place in 2012 for the cryptocurrency known as Mastercoin. The ICO actually took the form of the whitepaper for the cryptocurrency which the creator released to the public and asked for a donation of one bitcoin, worth about $100 per unit at the time, from anyone who felt that his proposal had merit. In exchange for their donation, those who bought in received 100 Mastercoins. The proposal worked and the creation of Mastercoin was funded with about $500,000. As of 2018, one mastercoin is worth about $4.20.

Understanding altcoins

Bitcoin is such a dominant force in the market that it is literally its own classification, there are bitcoins and then there are every other type of cryptocurrency which are collectively known as altcoins. ICOs are the birth of altcoins. Bitcoin still encompasses a large market share of the cryptocurrency market cap which makes even the other big names in the space, feel like chump change, however it is far from perfect which called for the need of altcoins. In order to ensure you make the right decisions when it comes to the cryptocurrencies that you move forward with investing in, it is important to first understand the need for altcoins in the first place.

The most important thing to understand when it comes to the need for altcoins is that while Bitcoin was the first cryptocurrency on the market, it was still very far from perfect and decidedly not designed for the level of use that it currently experiences on a regular basis. A new block in the Bitcoin blockchain can only be produced once every 10 minutes, and currently, there is so much of a backlog that even if no new bitcoin transactions took place until things were caught up, it would still take nearly two weeks for things to finish processing.

Another issue that was not taken into account in the early days was the potential energy drain from the proof of work mining model when it is used on such a large scale. The extreme demand for these services means that each transaction now requires roughly the same amount of energy as it takes to run the average American home for nearly 48 hours. Finally, it is important to keep in mind that bitcoins are a finite resource. There will only ever be 21 million bitcoins in existence and a majority of those were mined in the early days of the cryptocurrency. These things were all conscious choices that the person who created Bitcoin, the alias Satoshi Nakamoto, made, based on usage case for their creation that was significantly less in scope than it has ultimately become.

While significant changes can still be made in the future like the Lightning Network, those who curate the Bitcoin blockchain have thus far proven extremely reluctant to do anything that would cause the value of those holding the greatest number of bitcoins to degrade. As these holds equate to several billion dollars in total, this is understandable. However, as the code that Bitcoin is based on is opensource, this leaves plenty of opportunities for others to come in and adapt the code in a wide variety of useful and interesting ways.

When it comes to looking for altcoins to invest in, it is important to look for those that improve on the core of the Bitcoin blockchain technology in a meaningful way either by improving the speed at which new blocks are created or by increasing its overall stability or security. Another option is to look for those that are operating on something different than the proof of work mining process that Bitcoin and a majority of the other cryptocurrencies on the market use. This is done either by changing the difficulty of the existing mining process or by authorizing the use of an entirely different type of verification system instead.

Due to the fact that there is such a wide variety of altcoins on the market, the possibility of falling for a scamcoin is surprisingly high as well. Scamcoins is the umbrella term that has been given to any altcoin that was created for no other reason than to profit the creators. You can never expect these types of coins to increase in value past their ICO and they are always a losing proposition unless you are in on the scam and are able to abandon ship the second the ICO is completed. It can be quite difficult to differentiate between a coin that is struggling to find its audience and a scamcoin which is why it is so important to do as much research as possible before you invest, while also ensuring that you never invest more than you can afford to lose in the process.

ICO breakdown

The average ICO starts with a set of data relating to the company and project in question:

- **Whitepaper** that serves to outline the budget and details of the project
- **Goals**
- **Unique aspects** of the project that set it apart from its competition,
- **Technical specifications**
- **General timeline** relating to when the project will reach the market
- **Release of coins** into the system.

Generally speaking, a new ICO sets aside a specific number of coins to be released before the start of the sale, though sometimes an unlimited number of coins are made available right from the start. Additionally, there may be limits on the number of coins that one person can buy at a time and the price that investors pay can be either fixed or set to fluctuate as investor interest increases.

While the idea here is that getting in early will practically ensure a profit of some sort as the price of the coin has nowhere to go but up, it is important to keep in mind that this is far from a sure thing and it is difficult to predict what the price is going to do once the coin is live in the wild. When it comes to the actual ICO event itself, they will typically take place through either a private website or a third-party company such as a public cryptocurrency exchange or via an escrow service to ensure that the process at least has some degree of legitimacy.

Do your homework

As a general rule, the most effect means of determining if a new cryptocurrency is worth investing in is to make sure that it has either been created with a specific application in mind, designed to do something that it is clear people want or to have altered the original blockchain code in a meaningful way. Essentially, you are going to want to ensure that it has a reason to exist besides the fact that it is a viable alternative to fiat currency as there are plenty of cryptocurrencies occupying that space.

One of the best places to start is to ensure that the ICO you are considering investing in is being offered by a team with a proven background in the cryptocurrency space and the industry in question. While a few years ago it was perfectly acceptable for a bunch of no-name individuals to put together something that would take the market by storm, these days much of the space has been codified and those that are working on the third generation of blockchain technology have already earned a proven track record coming up through the ranks of generations one and two.

While you may not be familiar with them, you can bet that those who are going to be investing will be looking for the previous superstars which means it will be extremely easy to attach names to previous success stories. On the other hand, you are also going to want to be on the lookout for altcoins whose team has no record whatsoever in the community as they likely do not have the experience to create something that is going to succeed in the long-term.

You can never tell what the future will hold

When it comes to choosing an ICO for the first time, it is extremely important to keep in mind that sometimes the market is going to move in completely unpredictable ways that no one could have ever, realistically predicted. For example, Dogecoin is a cryptocurrency that held a successful ICO in 2013. Its coin, the dogecoin, is emblazoned with the likeness of the Siba Inu dog from an internet meme that was popular at the time. It broke all expected records in its first month of crowdfunding and currently, there are plans to send a gold dogecoin to the moon in 2019. While it was designed as a joke, which explains the logo, it rapidly developed an impressive following and a market capitalization of greater than $60 million.

Dogecoin is different to many other cryptocurrencies in that it has a very rapid production schedule. 100 million coins were created in the first 18 months and millions more are added to the market each year. It is primarily used as a means for those who read social media posts to tip the content creators who provide particularly useful or thoughtful content.

When it was created, it was done as a joke, and those who funded it did so as a joke as well. Nevertheless, at its height, it was one of the most profitable cryptocurrencies on the market and there are likely multiple people out there who have since made a career out of cryptocurrency investment based on the $100 they threw at a joke based on a meme they had seen online.

This is not to discredit dogecoin or altcoins in anyway, it is simply to say that when you invest in an ICO you are taking a significant risk as it is very difficult to tell what direction the market is going to develop in early enough to ensure that you get in early enough to still turn a profit in the long run. Never forget, many parts of the cryptocurrency market may as well be the Wild West which means that sometimes you will just have to expect the unexpected.

Blockchain basics

For those who are unaware, blockchain technology was created at the same time as Bitcoin and is at the heart of all cryptocurrency technology. It is essentially a decentralized ledger that allows for the simultaneous storage of data from users spread out all around the world. Each blockchain is made up of individual blocks that are filled with unique information as well as information related to where they exist on the chain, making it easy for data to stay in order regardless of when, or where, it is uploaded to the rest of the chain. All of this data is timestamped and also secured in such a way that it is virtually impenetrable using existing technology.

The benefits of such technology extend far beyond simple financial transactions and into virtually every industry and every market worldwide which is why there are those who are pushing to make it work at virtually every level in new and exciting ways. While it is already synonymous with cryptocurrency payments, there is still more that can be done when it comes to facilitating the needs of businesses to ensure that blockchain technology is being utilized to its full potential.

One group that is working to ensure that this is no longer the case is the Ethereum Enterprise Alliance which is a group of corporations including Microsoft, JP Morgan, and Samsung that are currently working together to create a variation of blockchain technology based on the Ethereum platform that provides businesses with a greater overall level of control that will make it easier for businesses of all sorts to use the technology on a regular basis moving forward.

It is also important to keep in mind that while blockchain technology offers an alternative to fiat currency, and thus traditional banking services, it is the only alternative for these types of services in many other parts of the world. For example, there are more people in Kenya with access to a bitcoin wallet than with access to indoor plumbing, simply because there is no other way for them to reliably access the types of banking services much of the world takes for granted. Connecting so many people to the online world, all at once, is sure to have significant ramifications for retailers worldwide as well.

Another cost of doing business that is frequently overlooked is fraud which cost business owners an estimated $20 billion in 2017. Broken down, this means that nearly 30 percent of all profits are going to end up going to deal with some type of fraudulent activity on average. Blockchain technology has the potential to decrease this amount substantially as it can make tracking digital identities far easier than was previously the case as its results are always going to be properly authenticated, irrefutable and immutable. If this type of system were to become widespread then it would make it much easier for everyone to remain safe and accounted for.

Finally, another facet of worldwide business that is sure to see serious benefit from blockchain technology is going to be the areas of supply chain logistics. Currently, the process of shipping products between various suppliers has proven to be a complicated mess of incompatible systems and unreliable human components. Blockchain technology streamlines this process from soup to nuts, making tracking even the most complicated transactions as easy as following a few numbers on a page. When products are delivered the required signatures can be obtained electronically automatically and everyone who is involved will have access to the data to prevent any additional confusion further down the line as well.

Chapter 2: Investing in ICOs

In this chapter you will learn...

- How to make smart ICO investments
- How to do your own research on new ICOs

Investing in established cryptocurrencies is a risky proposition, and thus investing in ICOs is even riskier. There are several different reasons that this is the case, though the biggest one is that the companies that frequently offer this type of incentive are barely up and running which means they are not going to have much to show in terms of prototypes, you will be lucky to get a business plan out of them most of the time.

Therefore, doing the right research is imperative. Every ICO should have a whitepaper, website and business plan to work with and you will come across many ICOs that cannot even show all three. Due to the fact that the company is unlikely to have anything concrete to show off to investors, you are naturally taking a risk simply by moving forward with this course of action. Additionally, it is important to keep in mind that just because an ICO is seeing a lot of positive action, there is nothing to say that this positive mindshare will continue until the product launches, especially if there is going to be a significant wait between the ICO and the launch of the altcoin.

The following should be considered when evaluating an ICO investment opportunity.

Consider the team

While a charismatic figurehead has thus far appeared to be a leading factor in the long-term success of a new ICO, it is important to consider the contributions of the team as a whole, especially when it comes to put your money on the line. As such, before you make a move you should have a clear idea of the resume of each and every member of the team in question, including the advisory board, to ensure that the team as a whole has a robust history when it comes the cryptocurrency market. While you likely will not know their names, it is important that the list of projects they have worked on include as many recognizable projects as possible, the more the merrier. The greater the number of successful projects the team has under its belt, the greater the odds of it actually seeing the light of day in a usable form.

Consider how the community is reacting. While not necessarily an indicator of long-term results, it is always a good sign when the ICO you are considering is picking up grass-roots buzz from the cryptocurrency community. The more people who are interested in the ICO's team and advisors before it starts, the more likely its team has trust with in the community. It is also more likely the allotted amount of cryptocurrency will sell out and that those who get in at the very start will already be turning a profit before the ICO is completed.

One of the most active forums online, when it comes to ICO conversations, is Bitcointalk.org. It is the biggest cryptocurrency forum online as of 2018, and any ICO of note is almost certainly going to have their own announcement thread there. When frequenting the threads surrounding new ICOs, it is important to look at each and every comment. These forum threads will often provide you with ICO details that will be unavailable anywhere else and also, frequently, give you the opportunity to talk to some of the team or advisors behind the ICO directly. Regardless, the type of buzz in the community will likely give you additional insight into how the cryptocurrency in question is likely to expand if it does catch on in the mainstream.

Overall, you can think of the forum thread as a type of microcosm of how the world at large will react to the ICO in general. This makes the negative comments just as useful as the positive ones because if you look past the banal comments you can find legitimate issues that people could put forth about the cryptocurrency in the future, which could hamper the efficacy of your investment significantly if it catches you off guard. Generally speaking, if the forum thread is not positive at this early stage of the game it is unlikely to improve much after the ICO launches.

It is important to ensure that this buzz is not artificially generated either, as ICOs have been known to offer coins to community members who make it seem as though there is an extra buzz surrounding the ICO in question known as 'shilling'. A popular tactic for new cryptocurrencies these days is to create a bounty on social media and forum posts that reflect positively on the ICO whereby they pay out in cryptocurrency for each and every piece of seemingly grassroots positive buzz that is added to the blogosphere.

The easiest way to see if this type of buzz is building is to search for the ICO in question with the word bounty after it. If there is a Twitter, Facebook or Reddit bounty on the ICO then this should be enough to find it. You should also be on the lookout for multiple people posting almost the same type of post as this can be a sign that all of those accounts are working from the same script.

Consider the current status

Before committing to investing in any new ICO, it is important that you take a look at the current state of the project as a whole. First, this means taking a look at the stage of the project, including the amount of capital that has been invested up to this point and how close the project is to launching with what they have already collected. Ideally, you will be able to look at a beta version of the product or service that is going to utilize the cryptocurrency in question, though projects that are this far along are typically few and far between.

Generally speaking, the whitepaper should be convincing with no spelling or grammatical errors with a credible request for funding. While taking on an investment at its early stages is practically the pinnacle of risk, if the ICOs in such a state comes to fruition and performs admirably the risk can be worth the reward for those with a mind to chase it. This is what makes ICO investing similar to investing in any other venture capital opportunity.

There are still going to be differences, of course, the most important of which is that investing in an ICO does not give you equity in the company. As such, it is all about finding the appropriate level of risk for you and then having the faith in yourself to understand when you have found a project that is worth moving forward on and being able to commit to it without reservation. In fact, there are several cryptocurrency venture capital firms currently in operation, including Fenbushi which is owned by Ethereum founder Vitalik Buterin. Seeing one of these names attached to an ICO should make you feel much more confident when it comes to making the investment.

Take the community presence into account

While an active community may or may not exist around the ICO or cryptocurrency in question, depending on the current state of the project when you invest, it is always important to track the growth of the community as time goes on. A community that is committed to the long-term success of the cryptocurrency can be extremely supportive during the early days and is thus crucial to ensuring that public interest grows during the critical early period.

Additionally, you are going to want to keep an eye on how communicative the developers are with their community, the more active the better. This will help to keep the community and the development team on the same page throughout the launching of the cryptocurrency, which can give you potential leads on future positive movement in the future as well. They should have a Telegram group, be active on Twitter and have their own dedicated website as a very minimum. Activity on Reddit and Facebook is an additional bonus. Above all else, you are going to want to ensure that the atmosphere of the community remains positive and that its number continues to move in a positive direction.

Ensure there is a demand for the service

When it comes to ensuring that the ICOs you back do not end up as just another shitcoin – a term actually used - the easiest way of going about doing so is to avoid any ICO that does not have a clear reason to exist. Specifically, if its whitepaper does not include both a pressing problem of the modern world, followed by a concise explanation of how the cryptocurrency in question can, and will, fix it, then you are going to want to pass on that ICO. Assuming the ICO gets this far at least, then the next thing that you are going to want to do is to do your homework and see what the demand is actually like out in the real world.

This means you are going to want to search online looking for people who have a pain or problem that the ICO hopes to solve, including checking out the frequency of such searches on Google. For example, if you were interested in investing in an ICO that creates a blockchain-based alternative to traditional dental insurance, then you would want to research the demand for such services as well as the likelihood that dentist would get on board.

In addition to ensuring that the goal of the cryptocurrency or blockchain project that you are funding is going to fill a real need, that real people are going to be interested in dealing with in a new way, it is important to ensure that the cryptocurrency itself is going to legitimately be a part of the process. This means you are going to want to consider the reasons that the project in question could not make do with an existing coin, and ensuring it is not just a way to line their pockets. After all, cryptocurrencies find their value based on supply and demand which means if there is no future demand for the cryptocurrency in question then your early investment will not mature in any real way.

Know the stats

While during the earliest days of cryptocurrency, the number of coins that would ultimately be created was not all that important, ICOs routinely sell out in 60 minutes or less these days, so knowing just what you are getting into is extremely important when it comes to ensuring that you do not miss out. There are two types of ICOs to be aware of, open cap and closed cap.

An open cap ICO ensures that anyone who is interested in participating in the process can buy as many units of the cryptocurrency as they have a mind to which means that anyone who is interested in getting in on the ICO can do so right away. On the other hand, in the end, it makes the supply of the given cryptocurrency far greater, which means that the price is going to start off lower, and also struggle to rise until more users come in to balance out the demand.

As the early days could easily be the only days the cryptocurrency ever makes money, this makes open cap ICOs a risky proposition, even by ICO standards. For example, the blockchain company Bancor ran an ICO in the summer of 2017 that raised $150 million in under three hours. Despite this impressive number, the investors at the time saw zero gain as the amount of cryptocurrency for sale was unlimited.

Alternately, if you invest in an ICO with a hard cap, then there are only going to be a set number of coins available for purchase and each investor is limited to a set number of coins. While this naturally means you need to be prepared to strike while the sale is on fast, the cryptocurrency has the potential to start building demand right away as supply is limited. By far the hard cap ICOs have the greatest potential. Anything below 600 million coins has good potential.

Be aware of the specifics of receiving your tokens

Before investing in an ICO, it is important to have a clear idea of just how you are going to receive your tokens, as well as the timeframe for the process to take place. This is because some projects are almost ready to release their cryptocurrency right away, while some have yet to even fully finish creating the blockchain that will house the cryptocurrency in the first place. While sometimes this can create additional hype around the project, which is what happened with Ethereum, this delay in momentum is just as likely to hurt the new project as it is to help it. Most tokens which are launched on the Ethereum blockchain are supported by My Ether Wallet which is a paper wallet solution. Visit www.myetherwallet.com

While the total number of coins that are being created is important, you will also want to pay special attention to the number of coins that are being made available to the public, compared to the number that are going directly to the development team. If the split appears to be in the team's favor, then you will need to carefully consider your investment as they may just be looking to make a quick profit and then discontinue the project, something that those who start ICOs can definitely do as there is little in the way of regulation around these types of transactions. No more than 50% of the coins should go to the ICO team.

As such, this is a great way to get a look at the true motivations of the team behind the ICO, regardless of how great their whitepaper might seem.

Consider the whitepaper: While this should not need to be said, studies show that less than 40 percent of all investors read the whitepapers of their investments completely, so it is worth repeating. Remember, this can be considered a roadmap of where your entire investment is going both in the short-term and the long-term which means that not reading through it thoroughly is akin to gambling with your investment capital.

It is also important to keep in mind that the scenario presented in the whitepaper is typically going to be the best-case scenario for the project, which means that it is important to be skeptical about any results that appear too good to be true. Even still, the details found in the white paper should be enough to give you the most important details regarding the project while also coming away from reading it with a clear idea of how its goals are going to be leveraged to solve the problem that was previously discussed as well. By the time everything is said and done, you should have a clear idea of the value that the project will bring to the world, how the team will reach their goals and how it is going to outpace the competition they may face in the market.

Know the code

While you do not need to be a programmer in order to invest wisely in ICOs, you will still need to read up on what programmers think of the source code for the project in question before you invest anything substantial. This should be a relatively straightforward process as blockchain code is traditionally released in an opensource format, going all the way back to the original Bitcoin blockchain that was released on GitHub.com.

If you visit the GitHub page for the ICO you are considering you should be able to easily find programmers commenting on the code. Again, you do not need to understand what they are saying, all you need to be able to do is gauge the overall response and ensure that it is positive in order to move forward with your investment with relative confidence. Again, you do not need to be worried about every single negative comment, just the trends that they appear to be creating as if 20 people comment on the same issue then maybe it is worth looking into. The people on GitHub likely have nothing to lose, they are simply commenting on the code as they see it which means they can be an extremely effective judge of the overall quality of a potential project.

Chapter 3: Mindset for Investing in ICOs

This chapter you will learn...

- Mental hurdles to overcome investing in ICOs
- External pressure

When it comes to investing in ICOs, the current wisdom often takes its cues from the cryptocurrency motto HODL. Short for hold on for dear life, the reverse acronym HODL first came into being in 2013 when an inebriated bitcoin owner posted on a message board that despite the recent drop in price he was planning on holding his bitcoins rather than cashing out before presumably all of the recent growth value was destroyed. The subject of his post was "I AM HODLING". HODL has since gone on to represent the idea that, due to its extreme volatility, it is often best to hold onto cryptocurrency through its dips as it will ultimately bounce back stronger than ever before. This is, of course, assuming that you have chosen wisely in the first place.

When it comes to dealing with ICOs, the decision to HODL will often come at the point where the ICO's cryptocurrency has launched successfully and you, as an investor, are now staring down its first significant price increase. The question then becomes whether to take your profits or continue holding in hopes of future gains and, it is rarely going to be black or white. The answer to this question will be formed starting with your overall aversion to risk. As investing in ICOs seemed reasonable to you in the first place, then you are likely more comfortable with risk than most; even still, however, there is still a range of risk levels that span a limited desire to protect your initial investment on one side and a desire to go all in for the biggest reward possible on the other. When it comes to making the right HODL decision for new ICOs, consider the following.

Start with the basics

Assuming you did your research and bought into an ICO for a useful company and find yourself faced with a potential windfall, the choice of cashing out or letting it ride in hopes of future gains can be a difficult and multifaceted decision. Generally speaking, the best place to start when it comes to determining the best course of action in the moment is going to be considering every aspect of your current situation. The first thing you are going to want to consider is the amount of debt, as there are few better ways of increasing your overall potential for profit in the future than by minimizing your debt as quickly as possible.

As an example, assuming you paid around $250,000 for your home via a loan that you paid 20 percent for up front, you can expect to pay about $5,500 in interest each year. As such, if you have 25 years left on your mortgage, you can expect to spend more than $100,000 purely in interest before things are said and done. If your profits are not quite at buying a home outright levels, you could still consider paying off your car, which will save most people about $1,000 per year in interest. The interest rate on credit card debt is typically around 20 percent per year as well which means the sure thing of clearing the debt is often going to be worth the potential loss of future income.

If you are already relatively debt free and are instead simply looking for a reliable investment plan, then you might want to consider a popular investment strategy known as compounding whereby you take your initial profits and reinvest them either in the same cryptocurrency when it decreases in value or in another cryptocurrency that you expect to see significant gains in the short-term.

For example, if you are currently 25 years old and want to save a million dollars by the time you are ready to retire at age 60, you would need to invest a little less than $900 per month, assuming you were going to maintain a steady five percent return on your investments for the next 35 years. On the other hand, if you wait to start investing until you are 35 then you will need to invest about twice as much to reach the same point. Finally, if you wait 20 years and do not start investing until you are 45, then you would need to save four times as much to reach your goal.

Look at the roadmap for the coin

When it comes to deciding if you should hold past the initial price boom, it is also very important to keep in mind the potential for locking in a loss if you continue to hold. While this will not always be a concern for ICOs that make it to launch successfully, if you invested in the last moments of an ICO on a cryptocurrency with a hard cap, it is possible that you paid more than the coin could be worth at a point in the future. If that is the case, then you should primarily be concerned with ensuring that your investment does not sour. If you do not see a profit it is ok to sell at the same price as you invested in to recover your money.

Assuming you are not accidentally locking in a loss, then the question becomes the amount of profit that you would realistically accept. When looking for this answer, you will need to consider the overall health of the cryptocurrency both in the moment and in the long-term. The most effective means of going about doing so is going to be through a process of fundamental analysis.

While technical analysis is the typical go-to for more established cryptocurrencies, those without a past will not have the types of patterns that are required to use it effectively which means that a more nebulous approach is often going to generate more productive results. Generally speaking, what you are going to be considering is the level of volatility you can expect from the cryptocurrency moving forward. While there are numerous types of volatility, the two that you are going to be focused on most regularly are historical and implied.

As the name implies, historical volatility looks at the amount of volatility the cryptocurrency has experienced up to this point. Everything else, specifically the current and future price, are broadly referred to as implied volatility. Implied volatility is often higher than historical volatility unless the early days of the new cryptocurrency have been especially perilous. When it comes to estimating volatility, consider the following factors.

Amount of press

While press leading up to the ICO can lead to higher than anticipated starting prices when it comes to determining the volatility of a currently active coin you will need to see what people are saying about the cryptocurrency in the moment to get the clearest idea of what is coming next. While stories about the price increasing rapidly, the currency being listed on a popular exchange or a successfully launched new feature can all be great for the price, the press can also be a negative influence on the price if these things go poorly instead.

This is especially true as there are so many different types of cryptocurrencies on the market that all it takes is a whiff of bad news before the speculative market turns on the cryptocurrency and prices tank as a result. While there are always going to be dips after significant increases as satisfied investors take their profits, it is important to have a good idea of the difference between this type of movement and a mass exodus based on bad news that you have not yet found out about. Knowing the difference will save you from being jumpy and making a mistake as a result.

Understand public perception

When it comes to determining the volatility of a new cryptocurrency, it is important to keep in mind the perception that the community growing around it has, as well as that of the greater crypto community as a whole. This is especially important during the earliest days of the coin when its total value made up of its perceived value, store of value and its means of transferring value are all in flux. A store of value is the function through which an asset will be useful at a future point and time with some level of certainty. A store of value can be either saved or exchanged for goods or services at a later date.

Value transfer, then, is any concept or object that can be used to facilitate the transfer of properties between individuals. The volatility that is inherent in all cryptocurrencies gives it a variable store of value along with a very efficient means of transferring value. Understanding the ways that this perception has already changed, and will surely continue to change in the future, is key to ensuring future changes do not negatively affect your bottom line.

Consider the potential for liquidation

Depending on the amount of the cryptocurrency in question that you own, when compared to the amount of the cryptocurrency in total, you may also need to keep in mind that difficulties may arise when it comes to selling off your holdings all at once. While this will not be a concern in most cases, if you own 10 percent of a given cryptocurrency or more you will need to be aware that it may be difficult to liquidate everything you have all at once without affecting the overall price enough to potentially affect your profits. As such, new cryptocurrencies can be thought of as similar to small cap stocks and this similarity will persist until adoption rates reach a mass scale. Until then, those with larger holdings need to carefully diversify to prevent serious losses.

Keep an eye out for major losses

While it can be easy to picture new cryptocurrencies as existing in a vacuum, in reality, this is not the case. This means that you are going to need to keep an eye on the strength of the market as a whole, because if the cryptocurrency in question launches in the midst of a bear market, then its price could never reach its full potential through no real fault of its own. This is simply due to the fact that what happens to the major players in the market is often reflected in the smaller altcoins as well. While this can be beneficial, such as when Bitcoin rose nearly $20,000 in a matter of weeks, it can also have a chilling effect on the market as a whole, such as when it lost most of that gain in the following months.

Unfortunately, while good news helps everyone, bad news hits smaller cryptocurrencies twice as hard as their larger relatives because it affects their volatility twice in a single go. First, by decreasing their available level of float and again by increasing the potential for lift which leads to even more artificial scarcity. This lift can be avoided, however, if the related new cycle is extremely negative, thus keeping float to a minimum. It is also important to keep an eye on any news that breaks about exchanges as well as this type of news can make investors nervous regardless of how well their own investments are doing.

Keeping an eye on the general flow of news will make it easier to determine where a perceived negative trend comes from. This is crucial to ensure that you understand when selling is the right decision versus moments where a severe downturn could have absolutely nothing to do with the cryptocurrency in question. Committing to a HODL strategy means not only understanding the difference between natural dips in the market and true negative movement but being able to act on this knowledge as well.

Think about the big picture

A growing trend in ICO development is cryptocurrencies specifically aimed at making it easier for those in third world countries to access traditional banking services. As these countries tend to have much higher rates of inflation than the fiat currencies of the home countries that are investing in, the extreme interest disparity has been known to affect volatility levels as well. To ensure you do not misestimate, it is important to keep in mind the level of volatility the cryptocurrency is experiencing in relation to its primary fiat currency as opposed to comparing it to your own fiat currency.

The benefit of this fact, however, is that it means that cryptocurrency can be traded in a practically frictionless environment, further making it attractive to those whose home countries naturally have higher levels of inflation. This is due to the fact that taking on the loan through cryptocurrency, even through a new cryptocurrency, is often worth the risk to many individuals, volatility and all, because the rates for doing so would be so high otherwise. Additionally, it allows those from other countries to see even larger returns than might otherwise be the case via the same process, starting with instruments of debt in their primary currency which then offsets much of the risk of exposure that typically comes along with increased inflation in a secondary market.

Keep an eye out for government oversight

According to the US government, for tax purposes, cryptocurrency is an asset rather than a currency. While a reaction to this news was inevitable, the way the market responded was actually surprising when it comes to the effect on volatility. While the fact that cryptocurrency was officially recognized was good news and generated positive price movements virtually across the board, the classification as the property was less than ideal overall.

The most important result of this ruling is that it makes it even more difficult for the average person in the US to get into ICOs in the first place by adding an entire additional layer of complexity to the process. It may also have a long-term chilling effect on many smaller cryptocurrencies as it will cause people to be less inclined to receive cryptocurrency payments if it means they have to deal with additionally complicated tax formulas, especially if the option to use a fiat currency is still readily available.

Tips for success

Choose the right targets: If you find that your chosen cryptocurrency is about to experience a period of higher than average volatility, then it is important that you take this into consideration when it comes to choosing your sell targets. If you are experiencing higher than average amounts of volatility then it is common for the market to skew in one direction, before it finds a new pattern that is strong enough to break through established levels of support or resistance. What this means is that if you have stop losses in play, it is crucial that you place them at a point outside where you believe this movement will be, so they do not trigger too early before things get going.

Watch your losses: If the market is experiencing high swings in volatility then you can counter this effectively if you work with smaller stops while at the same time combining them with larger selling orders. This is an especially reliable strategy if it is used during periods where the market is ranging to an extreme degree. This strategy is riskier than some, but the resulting profits will be larger when things go your way making them even out in the long run. As it does require a greater than average level of risk, it is important to always have very clear expectations for the market before implementing this type of action.

Utilize leverage: Once your chosen cryptocurrency actually makes it onto an exchange, you will have the possibility to buy in above your means using what is known as leverage. While virtually all exchanges offer leverage as high as 20 to 1, this does not mean you should take advantage of it carelessly as it can cause great loss just as frequently as it does great rewards. Especially given the fact that new cryptocurrencies can experience as much as 25% volatility per day, you can lose your short before you even know what is happening if you are not careful when investing.

While a little extra leverage might not seem like a big deal while you are in the black, it is important to keep in mind that it is entirely possible for the average new cryptocurrency to move 100 points or more in a matter of hours which can lead to serious losses if you're invested heavily in a leveraged position. Even if you are using just three percent leverage on the trade, it does take an expert to see how the losses could add up far quicker than you could dig yourself out from under them. This makes it easier to see that not adjusting your leverage properly will leave you open to more than just losses, it can cripple your potential for profit significantly due to all the time you will need to spend making a profit just to break even.

Be prepared to diversify: While it can often make sense to hold onto a new cryptocurrency despite early trepidation. However, if you want to ensure the investments you choose are always moving in the right direction you will need to ensure there is enough diversification in your portfolio as well. This means that you will want to split your investment capital among somewhere between five and seven different ICOs to more or less mitigate the risk that each of them will add to your overall risk amount. The fact is that you should be ready to lose six of your seven investments and plan for that one winner to make up for your losses and more.

Chapter 4: Paying Taxes on Your Profits

In this chapter you will learn...

- Cryptocurrecies, ICO & taxes

As previously mentioned, due to a ruling by the IRS, cryptocurrency is considered an asset as opposed to a currency. This has made the process much more complicated than it otherwise may have been, which unfortunately causes many people to ignore the problem in hopes that it goes away. Those who ignore this aspect of investing in cryptocurrency for too long may find themselves seriously regretting it when the IRS comes calling. Specifically, when it comes to cryptocurrency you are going to want to concern yourself with IRS Notice 2014-21.

While the details gets rather dense, the broadest reaching application of this notice is that it lists cryptocurrency as property as opposed to currency. As such, even those who only ever use cryptocurrency for transactional purposes are considered investors by the federal government which makes paying taxes on their holdings much more complicated than it would otherwise be. What this means, above anything else, is that you should always speak with a tax adviser to make sure you are following all the relevant laws as closely as possible.

Losses or gains

One of the best parts of this decision is the fact that gains that are tallied in the longer term are taxed at a rate akin to capital gains rather than at a rate similar to other types of income which can work out to as much as 10 percent total savings when compared to the alternative. Even better, this change reflects a positive marginal rate as a result. If you sell in the short-term, however, the capital gains rate will be based on a standard income rate instead.

While it can be useful in some cases, being classified as property makes it far more difficult to write off losses that come from a profitable ICO than it might otherwise be. One of the biggest reasons this is the case is the fact that the yearly tax limit when it comes to property losses is only $3,000 regardless if the filing is for a single individual or a joint filing. This limit has remained the same since the 1960s and it means that even a mild ICO related loss would likely need to be carried forward multiple years just to ensure that everything evened out. This is a significant disadvantage when it comes to the way losses are handled on the foreign exchange market where such things can be taken at a one-to-one basis.

Furthermore, it is also important to understand that while capital gains taxes can be calculated in a relatively straightforward matter, with the property it becomes more difficult to accurately determine base costs as well. This is primarily due to the problems that crop up when it comes time to calculate the fair value on an asset that changed the price by up to 15 percent on the day that you purchased it. Luckily, the IRS provides a fair amount of wiggle room when it comes to reporting your purchased price. Specifically, you are allowed to use any price from the date of purchase as long as you use the same measurement for all of your filings for the year. What this means is that you are free to use the high, low or median for the day as long as you use stick with the same metric for all of your files. As such, as long as you are aware of this fact when you purchase your cryptocurrency you can use it to your advantage in the long run.

While theoretically, this works out so the fair market value for the buyer is the same as that of the seller, things rarely work out so smoothly as it is practically impossible to determine if things work out in this way as the technology for doing so is not readily available with so many different unregulated exchanges operating in tandem. Until such a method is developed it will remain virtually impossible to determine a true fair cost by any means better than estimation.

While the previously nebulous connection between cryptocurrency returns and taxes meant that many early investors were able to get out without paying much, if anything, to the IRS. These days are over, however, and the IRS has indicated that it is ready to get its share of the pie as well. This means that the 2018 tax season will mark a noted change to the previous policy of tolerance. For example, in 2013 only 802 people listed bitcoin transactions on their taxes; however, during that same period Coinbase reported significant gains and losses during the period, though, the cryptocurrency rose from $13 per coin to more than $1,100 each the IRS subsequently announced a large-scale investigation into Coinbase customer accounts, but then later scaled back the investigation to only focus on large transactions of $20,000 or more.

Convertible currency

One key distinction that was made by the Financial Crimes Enforcement Network was the difference between convertible and non-convertible cryptocurrencies. A convertible cryptocurrency can be thought of as one which has a real-world exchange rate that is relatable to the USD such that it could be considered as a substitute for real currency. When this definition was put forth, it essentially meant that Bitcoin was a convertible currency and everything else was in the clear.

Over time, however, the definition of what is and what is not a convertible cryptocurrency becomes far more complex. For example, based on the IRS decree, a virtual currency that is listed on an established exchange long enough to have a viable market value would it then be considered a convertible currency? If cryptocurrencies that are converted to fiat currencies are considered fair game, what, then, of those that can be converted into other cryptocurrencies, would they then be classified as convertible, and thus taxable?

Furthermore, as convertible cryptocurrencies are also retroactively taxable, if a cryptocurrency that is not convertible, such as one that is first released after an ICO, then becomes convertible at a later date, are you then responsible for a cryptocurrency that you no longer own if you made a profit when selling it? The short answer is that the only way the market will ever find answers to these questions will be when the government makes some important decisions in the space.

Cost base

To complicate things even more, cryptocurrency traders are provided with the ability to calculate their base costs using several different methodologies which allows for agency when it comes to choosing the one that is the most valuable. Due to the fact that they are classified as personal property, cryptocurrency investors are given the option of selling their assets based on either a Last-In-First-Out (LIFO) model or through a First in First Out (FIFO). They are also given the opportunity to sell off individual lots that are based on specific share identification methods that are similar to those found on the stock market.

Each of these options can then have serious impacts on the calculations that determine capital gains both in the short and the long-term. Essentially what each method lets you do is sell off units of cryptocurrency that are purchased at different periods of time. For example, if you first purchased equally units of Ethereum when it was worth $0.50 and then again when it was worth $50, the amount of profit that you would be taxed on would be dramatically different between the two lots of units assuming the current price was not at $500 even though the total amount of fiat currency traded for Ethereum would be the same regardless.

As such, when it comes to choosing an exchange to operate through it is important to be aware if they are using a system that automatically defaults one way or the other, or if they offer the option to choose between lots in this fashion at all. If this option isn't readily available, then you can simply set up different wallets for different lots of cryptocurrency. While it will require additional work on your part, when the time comes it will make selling significantly easier.

Conclusion

Thank you for making it through to the end of *Cryptocurrency ICO Investing: A Guide to Understanding ICO Investing*. Hopefully, it was informative and able to provide you with all of the tools you need to achieve your goals, whatever it is that they may be. The cryptocurrency market as a whole, and ICOs especially are an exceedingly new and everchanging market which means that becoming a lifelong learner is the only way to truly be successful in either the short or the long-term.

Additionally, it is important to approach ICO investing, regardless of the manner in which you are doing it, with an understanding that while it is possible for some people to make millions overnight, they are, far and away, the exception rather than the rule. If you go into ICO investment with the expectation that you will be able to retire from your first ICO, then not only will you be disappointed, you will likely make mistakes based around your misestimation of the market as well. You will see far more success if you treat your first investment as a stepping stone to bigger and better things in the future. Remember, investing in cryptocurrency is a marathon, not a sprint, slow and steady wins the race.

This is not to say that you should sit on the idea of investing in ICOs for a prolonged period of time, as each day brings the world closer to a period of cryptocurrency mass adoption. Once a large part of the population uses cryptocurrency on a regular basis, the market is going to stabilize and a vast majority of the 1,000 plus cryptocurrencies on the market will cease to exist, taking a vast majority of the potential profits along with them. The market is red hot as of spring 2018, but it will not remain that way forever, make your move or you will regret it.

Finally, if you found this book useful in any way, a review is always appreciated!

FREE eBook Available
This is my FREE GIFT to YOU

Click on the link below to collect your FREE GIFT & Avoid the 5 Deadly Mistakes

http://eepurl.com/c9Lsr9

BITCOIN

UNDERSTANDING BITCOIN, MINING, INVESTING & TRADING FOR BEGINERS

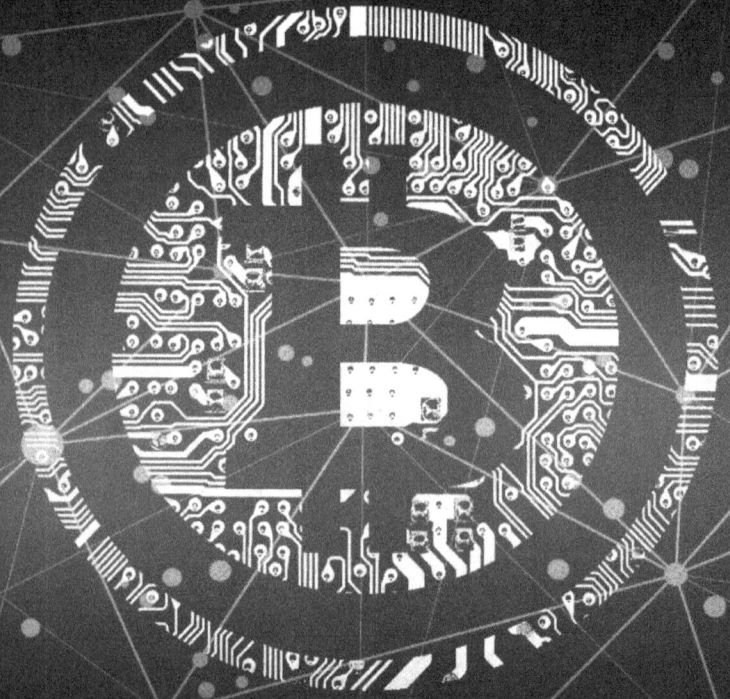

THE CRYPTOMASHER SERIES
SEAN BENNETT

www.ingramcontent.com/pod-product-compliance
Lightning Source LLC
Chambersburg PA
CBHW030059230526
45471CB00003B/1168